LET'S WORK IT OUT™

How to deal with HURT FEELINGS

Rachel Lynette

PowerKiDS
press™

New York

Published in 2009 by The Rosen Publishing Group, Inc.
29 East 21st Street, New York, NY 10010

First Edition

Editor: Joanne Randolph
Book Design: Kate Laczynski
Photo Researcher: Jessica Gerweck

Photo Credits: Cover, p. 1 Shutterstock.com; p. 4 © Yellow Dog Productions/Getty Images; p. 6 © Jesco Tscholitsch/Getty Images; p. 8 © Fat Chance Productions/Getty Images; p. 10 © iStockphoto.com/Anna Grzelewska; p. 12 © Shannon Fagan/Getty Images; p. 14 © iStockphoto.com/Galina Barskaya; p. 16 © Ethan Izzarelli/Getty Images; p. 18 © Tony Anderson/Getty Images; p. 20 © iStockphoto.com/Carmen Martínez Banús.

Library of Congress Cataloging-in-Publication Data

Lynette, Rachel.
  How to deal with hurt feelings / Rachel Lynette. — 1st ed.
     p. cm. — (Let's work it out)
  Includes index.
  ISBN 978-1-4042-4522-8 (library binding)
  1. Emotions—Juvenile literature. I. Title.
  BF723.E6L96 2009
  158.2—dc22
                                              2008009701

Manufactured in the United States of America

CPSIA Compliance Information: Batch #WW10PK: For Further Information contact Rosen Publishing, New York, New York at 1-800-237-9932

Contents

Josh felt bad that he had not played much in the game. He tried to remember that not everyone could play in every game.

What Are Hurt Feelings?

Katie got a new pink bag with kittens on it. She picked it out herself. When she wore it to school, Maya said that kittens were for babies. Katie felt sad. Maya had hurt Katie's feelings.

Having hurt feelings means you are feeling bad because of something that someone else said or did. People get hurt feelings for many reasons. Name-calling and teasing cause hurt feelings. People often feel hurt if other people do not like them. People may get hurt feelings if they are left out of a game or activity. When have you had your feelings hurt?

Brothers and sisters sometimes fight and hurt each other's feelings. Try not to do something you will feel bad about later.

Why Do We Hurt Each Other?

People often hurt each other's feelings when they are angry. When people are angry, they may say things they do not mean. Emma was drawing a picture when her little sister spilled milk all over the table by mistake. The picture was destroyed. Emma got angry and called her sister a mean name.

Sometimes, people hurt other people's feelings because they do not feel good about themselves. They may think that putting someone else down will make them feel better. Derek got teased at school. When he got home, he said mean things to his little brother.

It is all right to feel sad when your feelings get hurt. Try to think of something good about yourself to help you feel better.

It's Okay to Feel Bad

If someone hurts your feelings, you may feel sad, angry, or **confused**. It is okay to feel bad for a little while. Spending too much time thinking about bad feelings only makes them worse, though.

How can you make yourself feel better? One thing that might help is to think about what happened. It may not be as bad as you thought. What can you learn from what happened? It can also help to remember that you are a good person with many talents. Sometimes, it helps to talk to a trusted adult, such as a parent, teacher, or **counselor**.

Try talking to the person who hurt your feelings. You will likely find that that person did not mean to make you feel bad.

What to Say

If someone hurts your feelings, try not to hurt that person back. That will only make the **situation** worse.

When you are feeling calm, it may help to talk to the person who hurt your feelings. When you talk to the other person, try to start sentences with "I felt." Try not to start sentences with "you made me feel." Katie used "I felt" statements to tell Maya how she felt. She said, "I felt sad when you said my backpack was for babies because I picked it out myself. I felt like you were calling me a baby."

Stop fighting and saying mean things to other kids. Be kind to others, and start making friends instead.

Hurting Someone Else's Feelings

If you hurt someone else's feelings, you might feel **guilty** or **ashamed**. It may help to remember that you are not a bad person. You may have just made a bad decision.

It can help to think about how you were feeling when you said or did a hurtful thing. Were you angry? Were you feeling bad about yourself? Maybe the other person did something that made you feel upset.

Even when you are angry, you are still **responsible** for what you say and do. When you have hurt someone's feelings, it is your responsibility to make things right.

It is best to wait until you are calm to talk to someone about how you feel. You want the talk to make you both feel better, not worse.

Talking It Over

To make things right, you will likely need to talk to the person who hurt your feelings. When you talk to that person, it is important to be calm and **respectful**.

Carl made raisin cookies to share with his class for his birthday. Shannon tasted her cookie and then threw it in the trash. Carl saw what Shannon had done. Shannon realized that she had hurt Carl's feelings. Shannon wanted to make things right. She explained to Carl that she did not like raisins. Then they both felt better.

Tommy was not ready to accept his friend's apology. He still felt hurt that his friend had said mean things about him to someone else.

Saying Sorry

When you talk to someone after you have hurt his feelings, you may need to **apologize**. When you apologize, you tell the other person that you are sorry for what you did. If the other person accepts your apology, you will both feel better.

Sometimes, the other person is not ready to accept your apology. He may still feel hurt and angry. Hurting someone's feelings is **serious**. Sometimes, it is not easy to **forgive**. Be kind and try not to hurt that person's feelings again. Be **patient**. Someday, he may be ready to forgive you.

When you feel good about yourself, it is easier to make friends. If you feel proud of who you are, it will be hard for someone else to hurt you.

Feeling Good About Yourself

It is important to feel good about yourself. When you feel good about yourself, you are less likely to hurt another person's feelings. It is also harder for someone to hurt your feelings. Remember, just because someone says something mean about you, does not make it true.

Jason was playing **goalie** for his soccer team. He missed a shot and the other team scored a goal. Allan told Jason that he was a bad goalie. Jason thought about it. Even though he missed one shot, he caught most shots. Jason was not a bad goalie.

Joseph felt bad when Steph said she could not come over after school. Steph explained that she had dance class, and Joseph felt better.

Think Before You Speak

One way to keep from hurting other people's feelings is to think before you speak. Ask yourself if what you are about to say is hurtful. If it is, you should not say it. Can you find a different way to say what you feel without being hurtful?

Carmen asked Julie if she liked her haircut. Julie thought it was too short. She was about to tell Carmen that, but she realized that it might hurt Carmen's feelings. She decided to say something different. Julie said that she thought that the bangs were cute. Julie told the truth without hurting Carmen's feelings.

Feeling Good Together

When people are treated with kindness and respect, everyone feels good and no one gets their feelings hurt. One way to treat other people with kindness and respect is to always treat others the way you would like to be treated. If you do not like being called mean names or being left out of an activity, then do not do those things to other people.

Remember, you are responsible for your own **behavior**. You get to choose what you say and do. You can make choices that make you and the people around you feel good!

Glossary

apologize (uh-PAH-leh-jyz) To tell someone you are sorry.

ashamed (uh-SHAYMD) Feeling bad because of something you did.

behavior (bee-HAY-vyur) Ways to act.

confused (kun-FYOOZD) Mixed up.

counselor (KOWN-seh-ler) Someone who talks with people about their feelings and problems and who gives advice.

forgive (for-GIV) To no longer be angry with someone who did something.

goalie (GOH-lee) The person who guards the net and tries to keep the other team from scoring goals.

guilty (GIL-tee) Feeling that you have done something wrong.

patient (PAY-shent) Waiting calmly for something.

respectful (rih-SPEKT-ful) Treating others in a way that shows you think highly of them.

responsible (rih-SPON-sih-bul) Having the duty of taking care of someone or something.

serious (SIR-ee-us) Important.

situation (sih-choo-AY-shun) A problem or an event.

23

Index

Web Sites

Due to the changing nature of Internet links, PowerKids Press has developed an online list of Web sites related to the subject of this book. This site is updated regularly. Please use this link to access the list:

www.powerkidslinks.com/lwio/hurt/